ADULT COLORING BOOKS

MANDALA

VOLUME 1

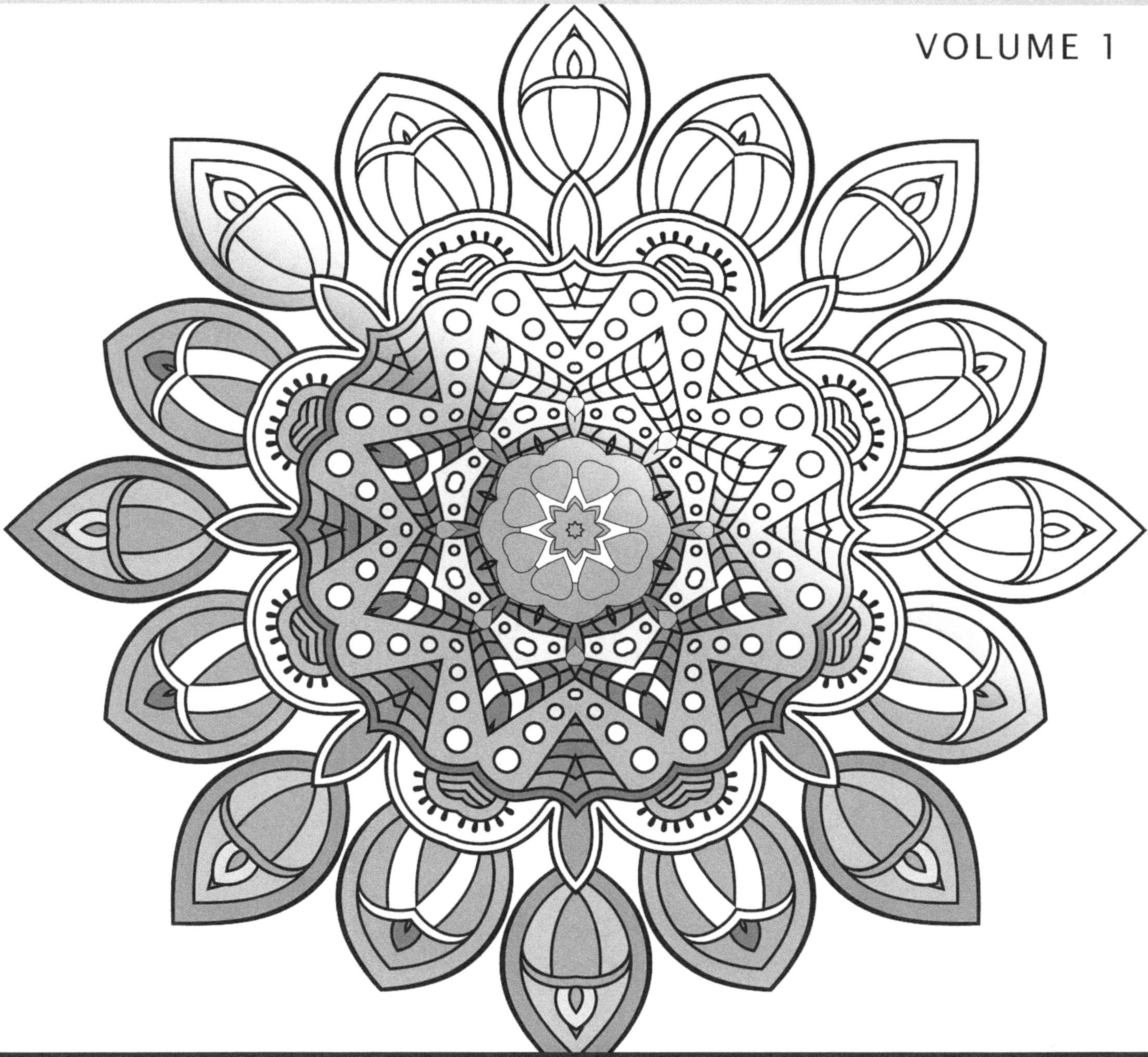

STRESS RELIEVING PATTERNS

COLOR TEST PAGE

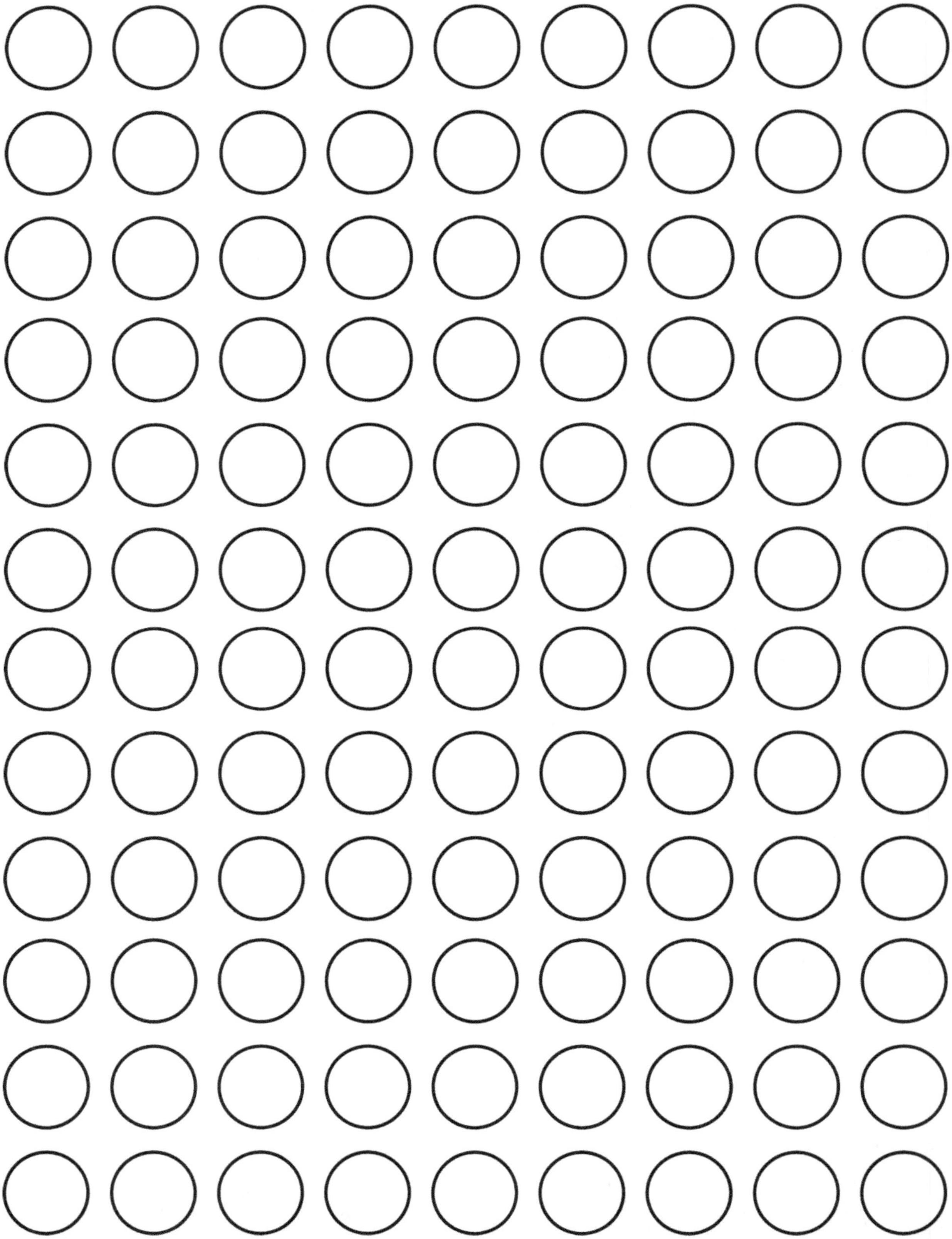

COLOR TEST PAGE

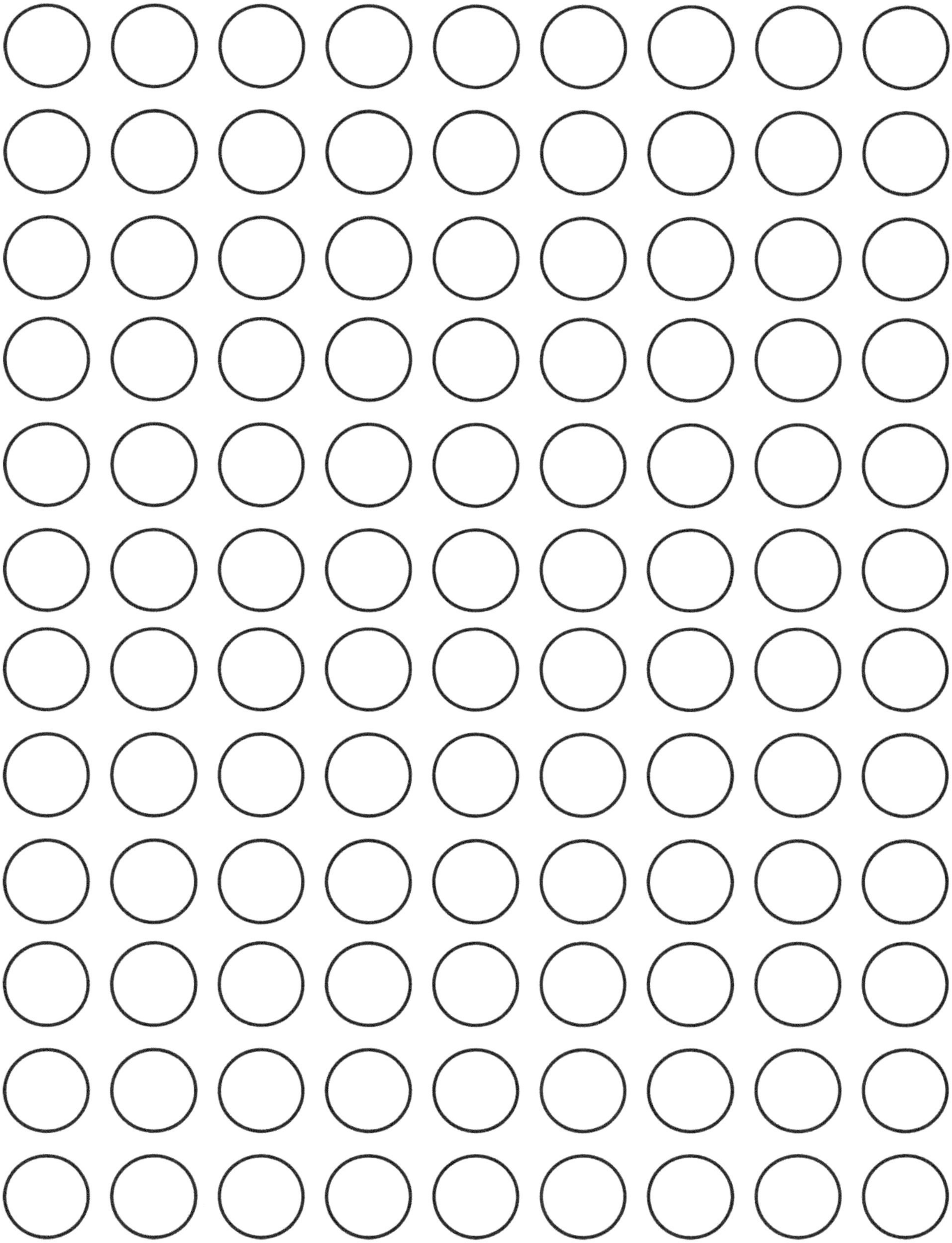

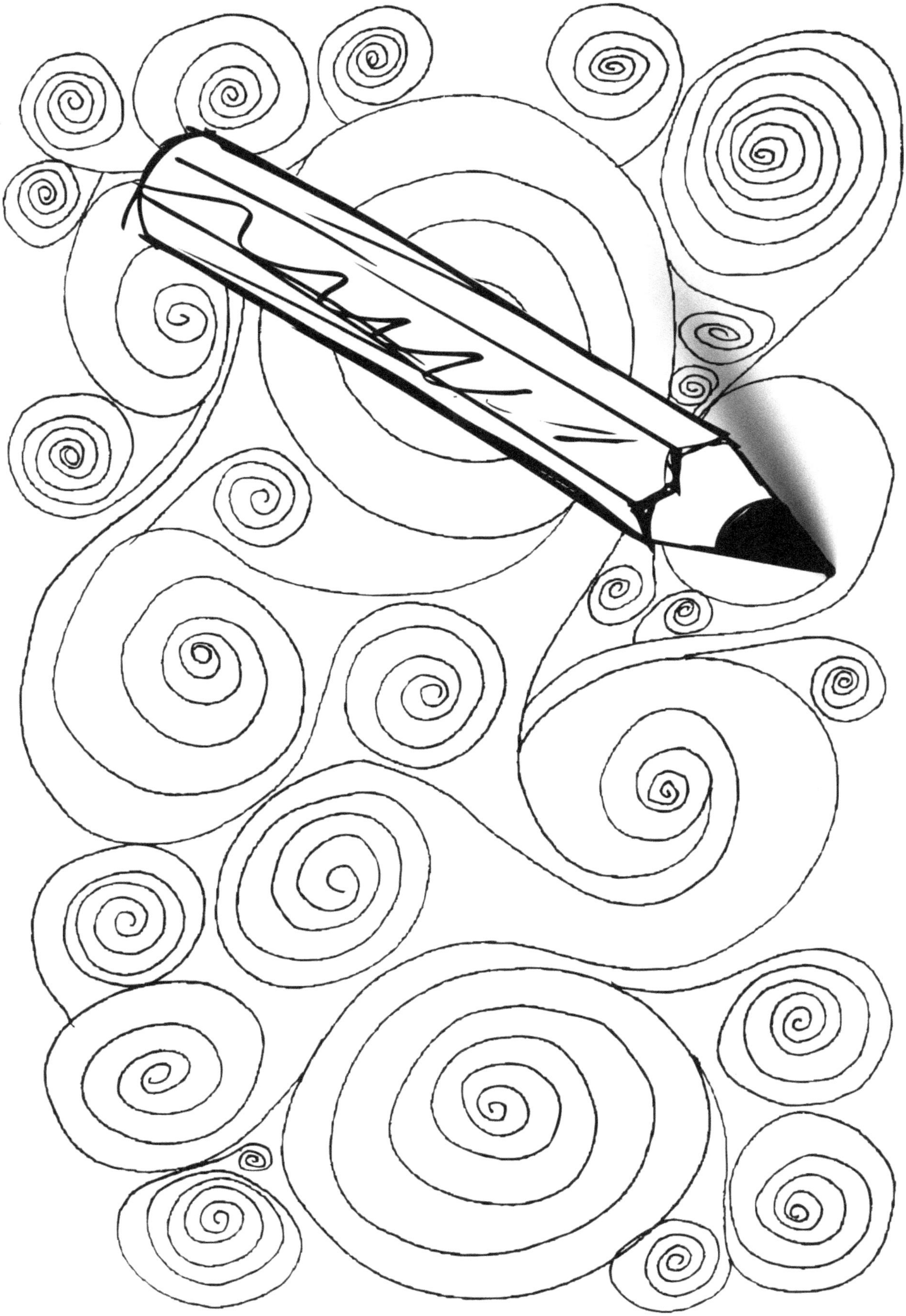

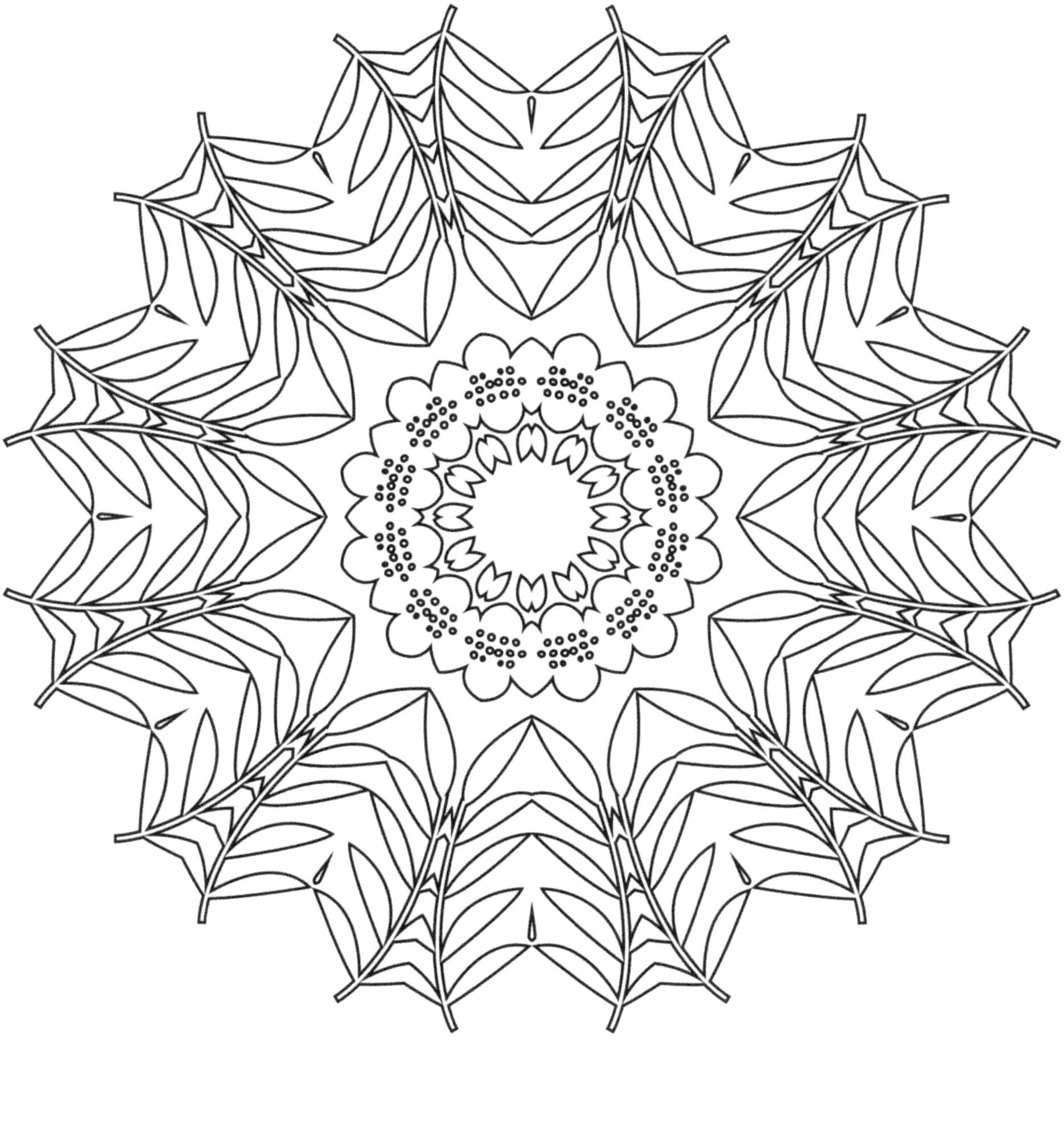

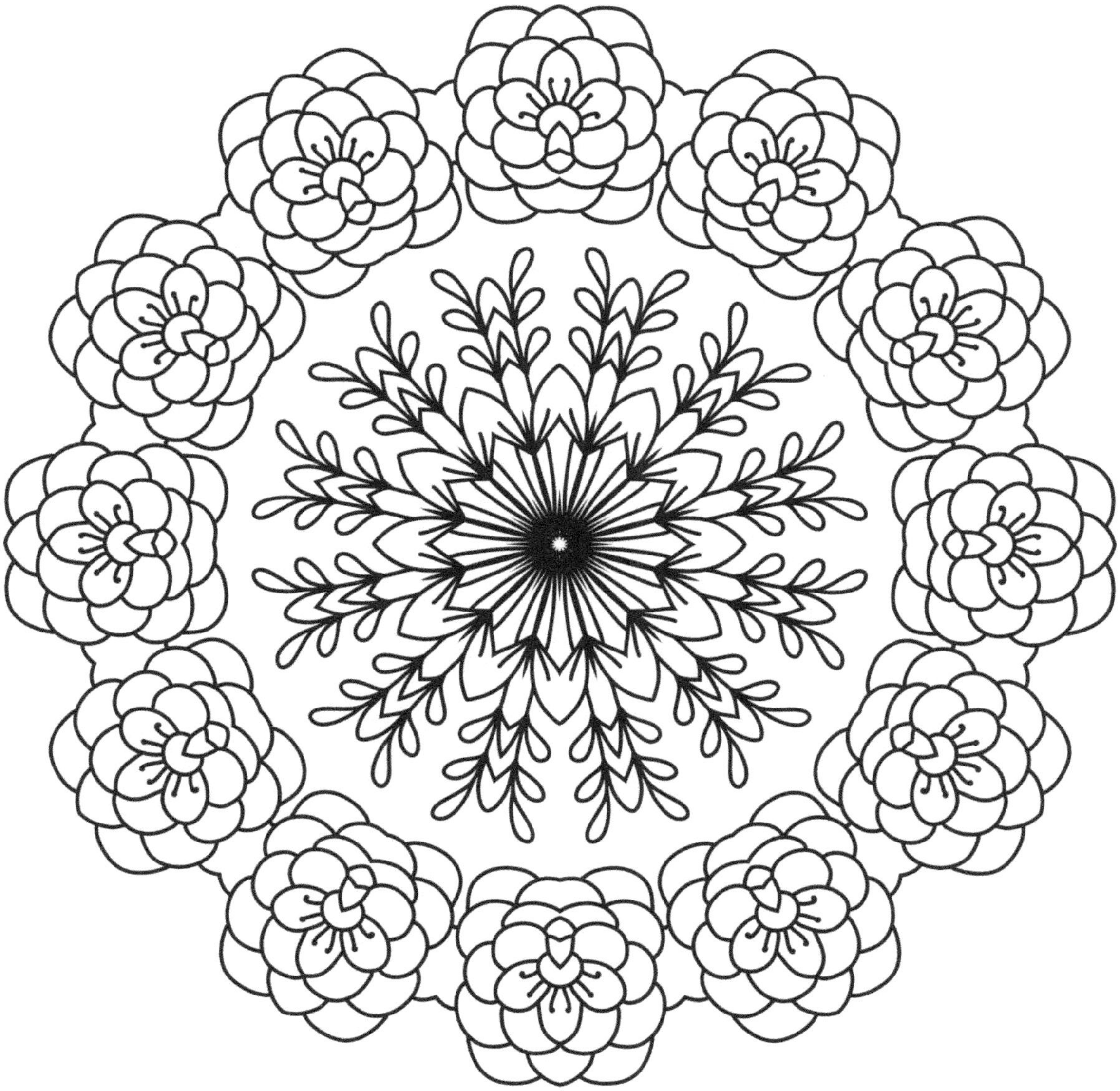

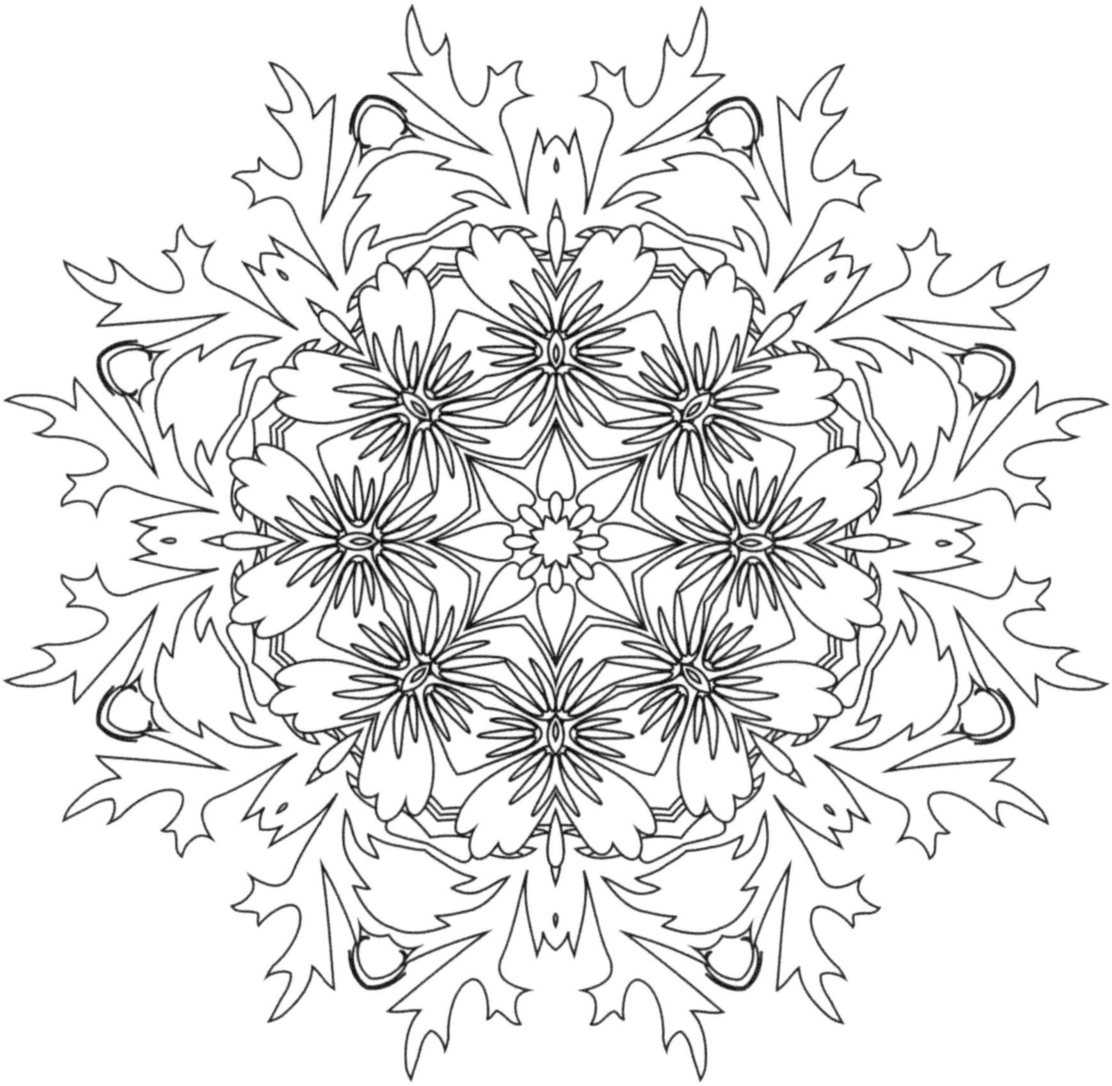

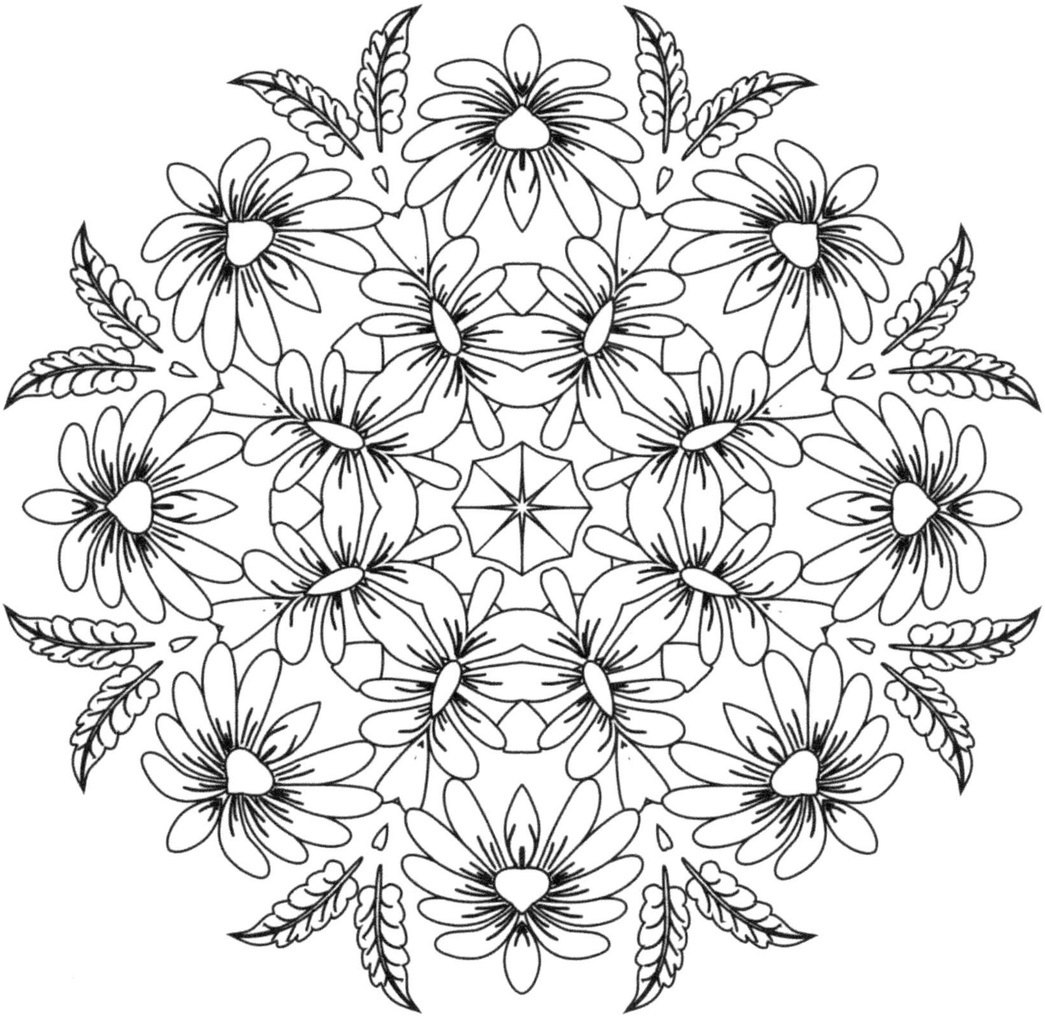

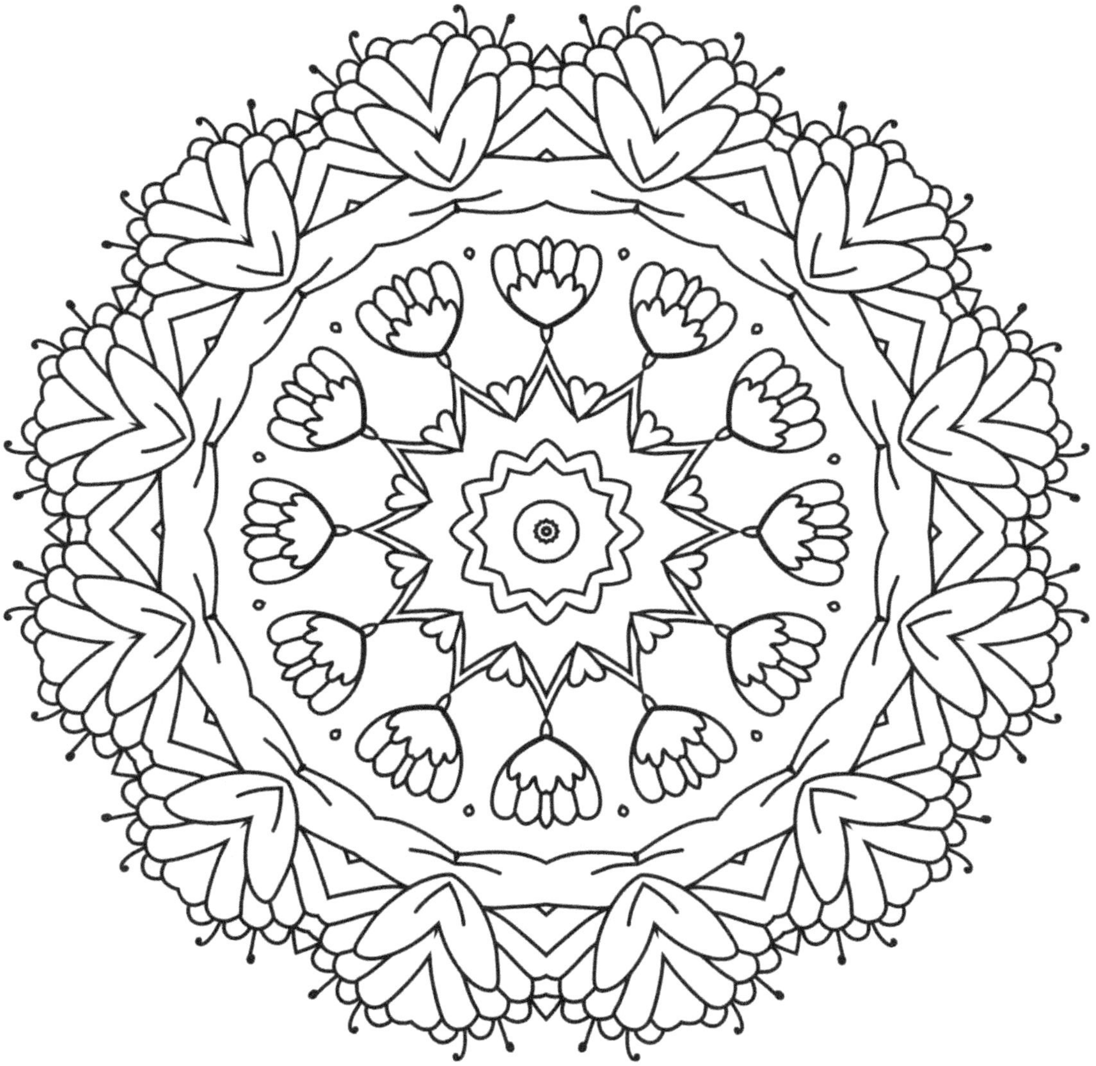

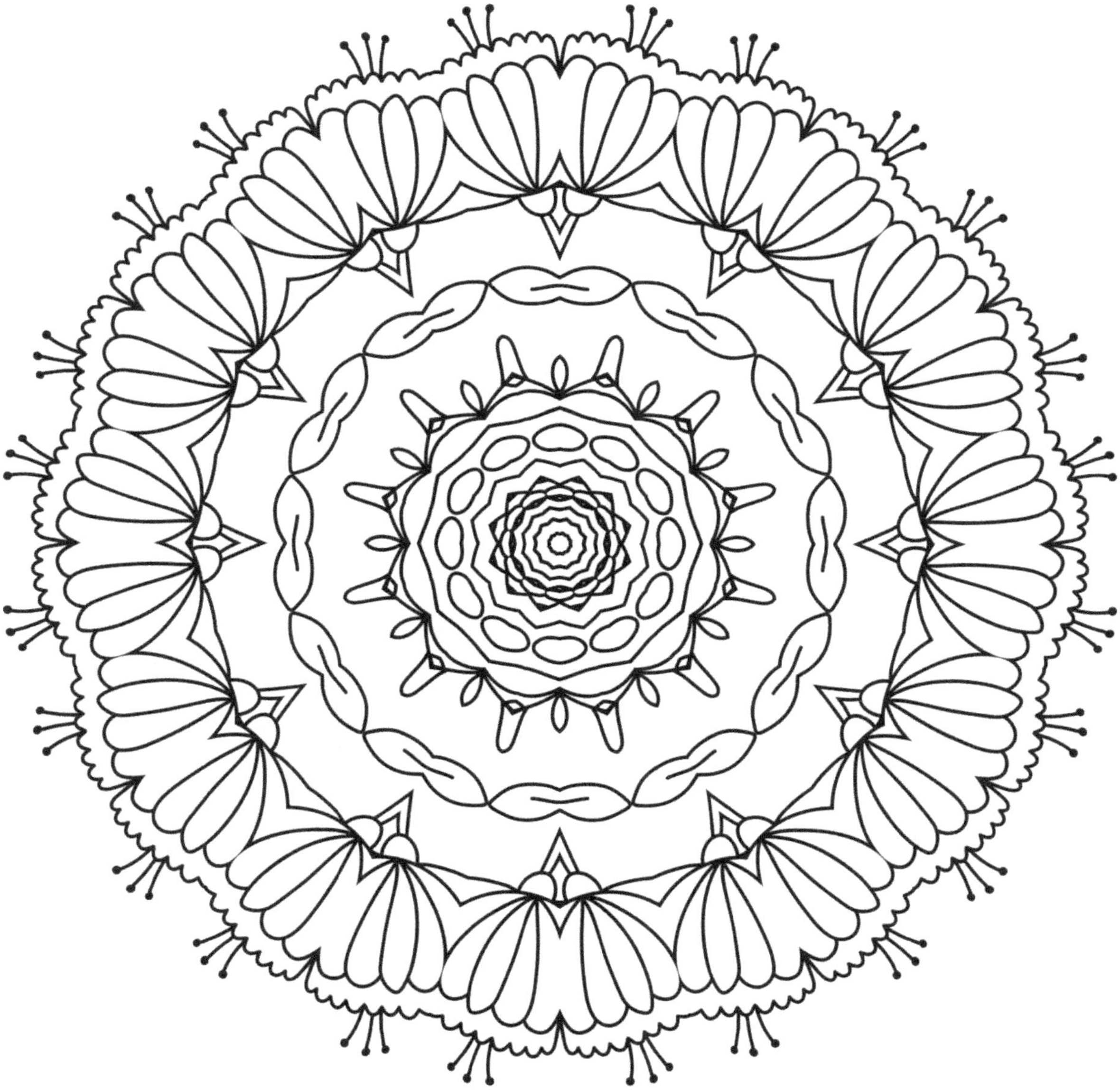

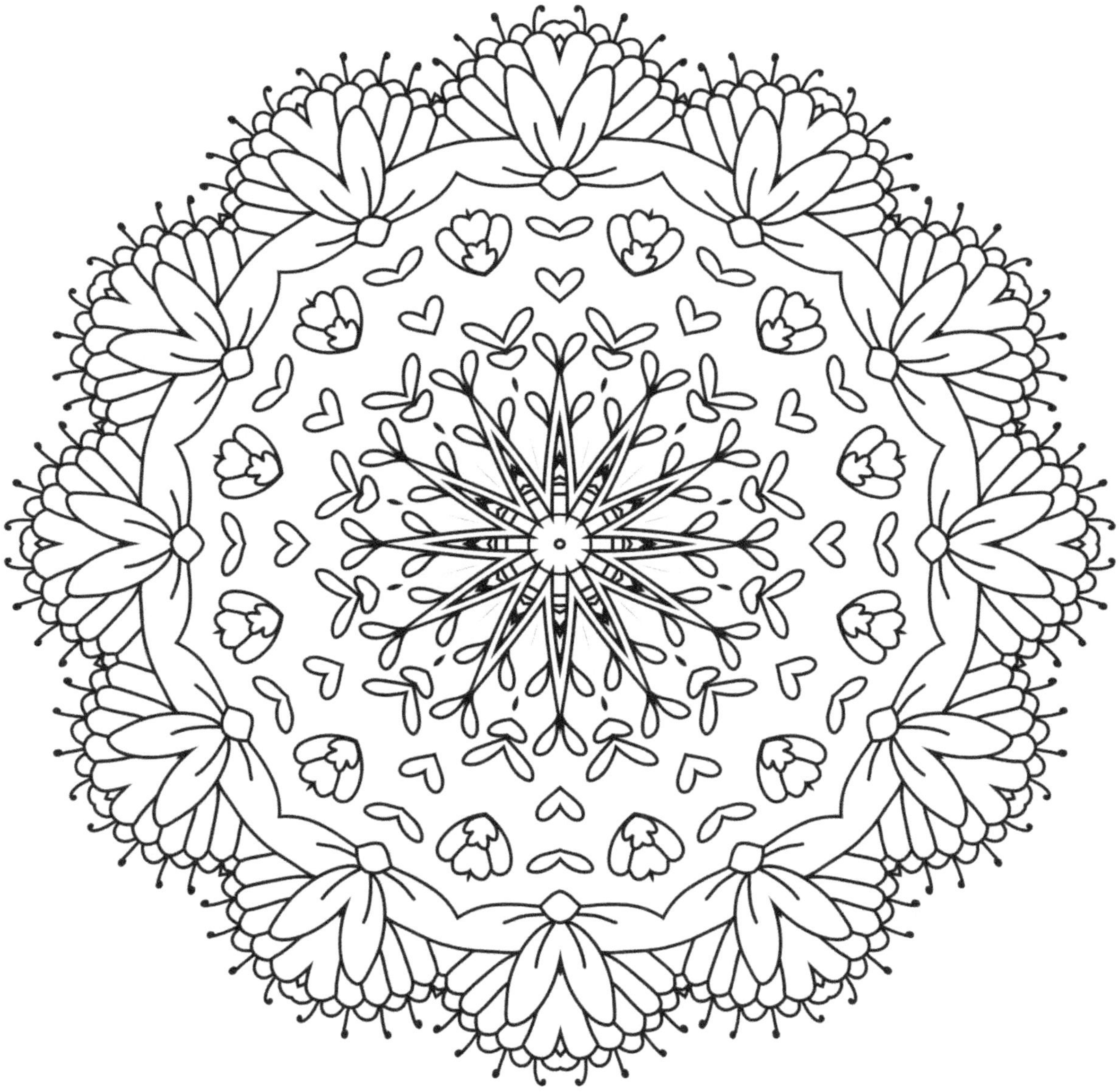

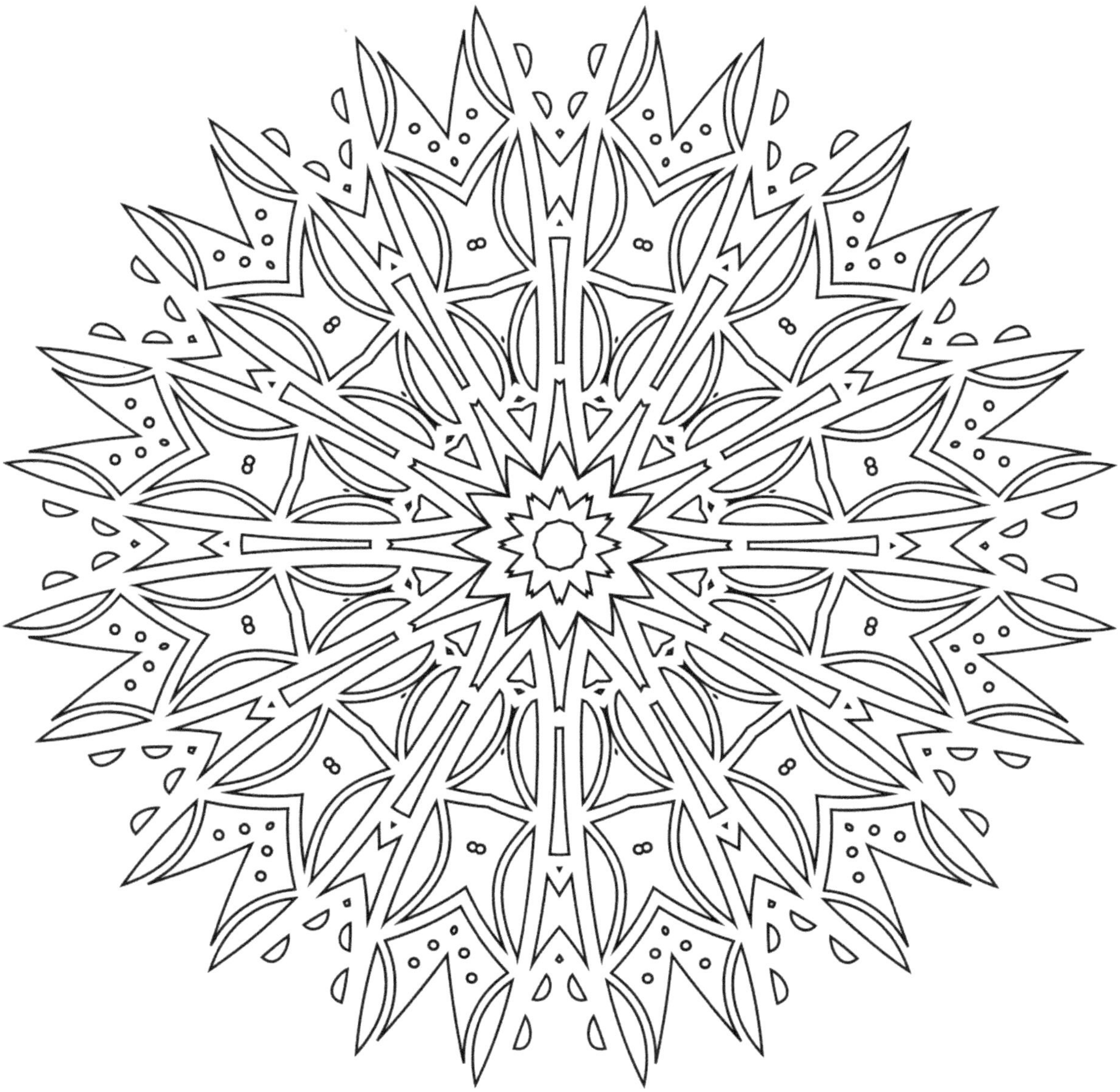

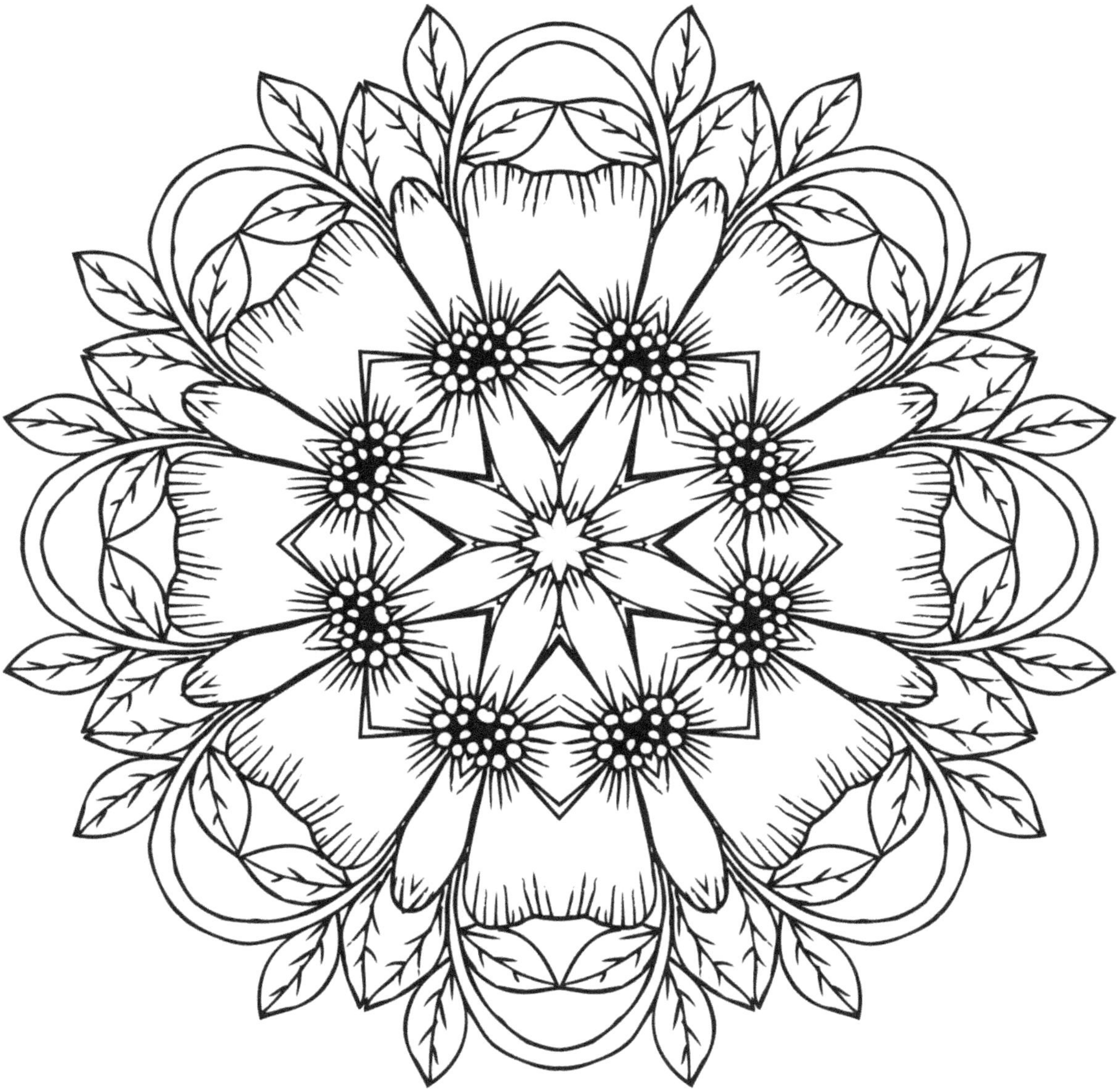

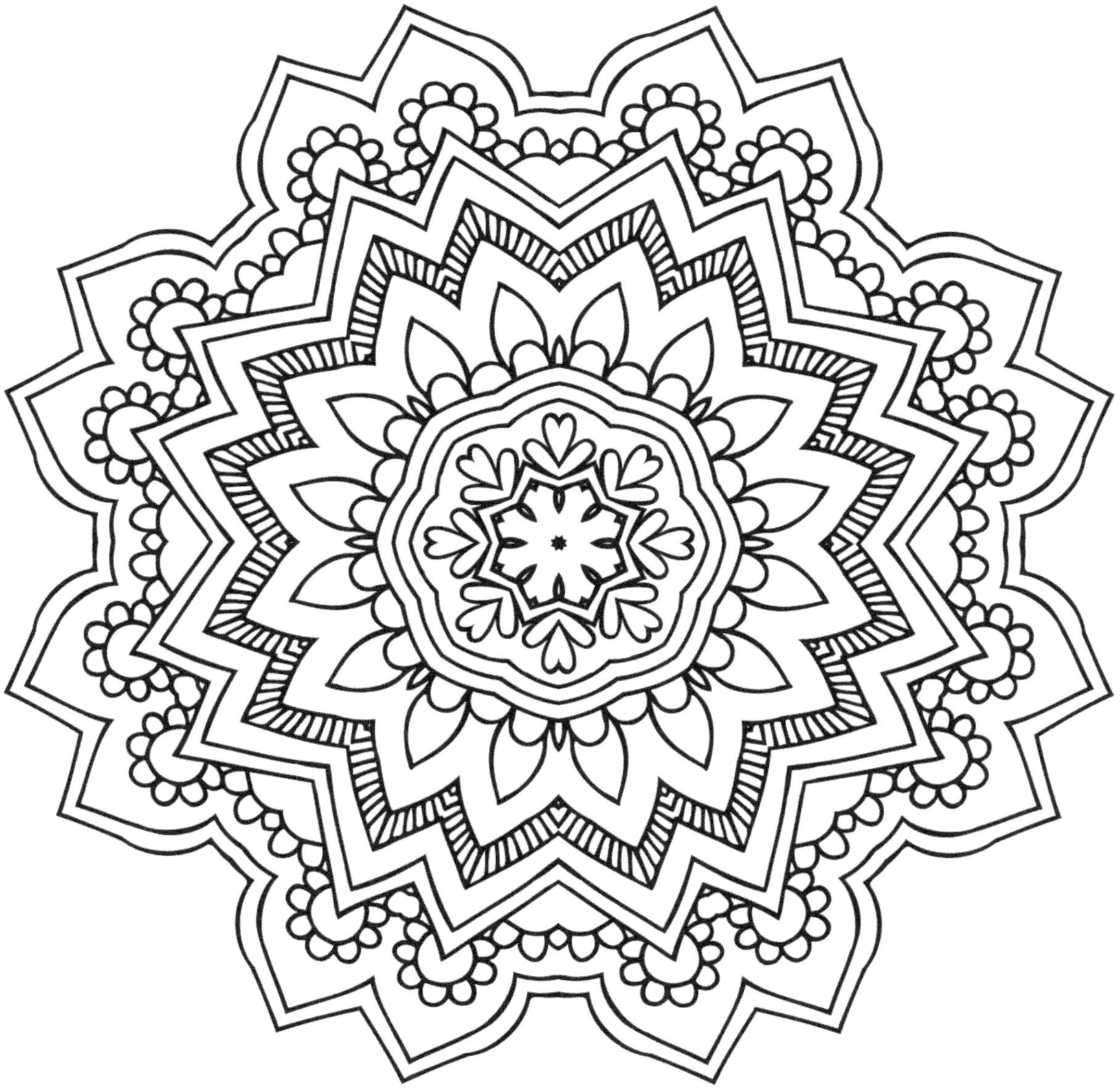

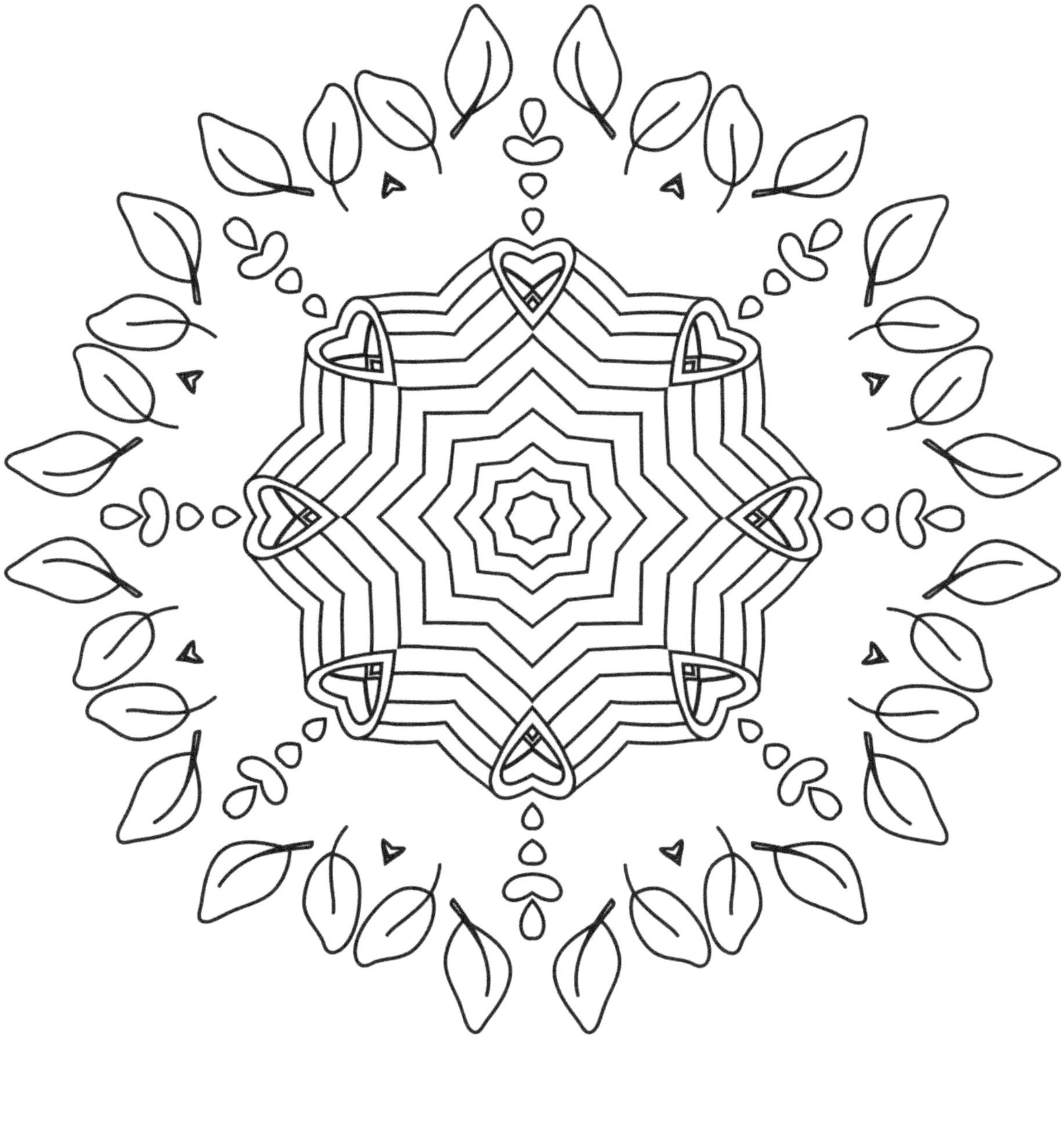

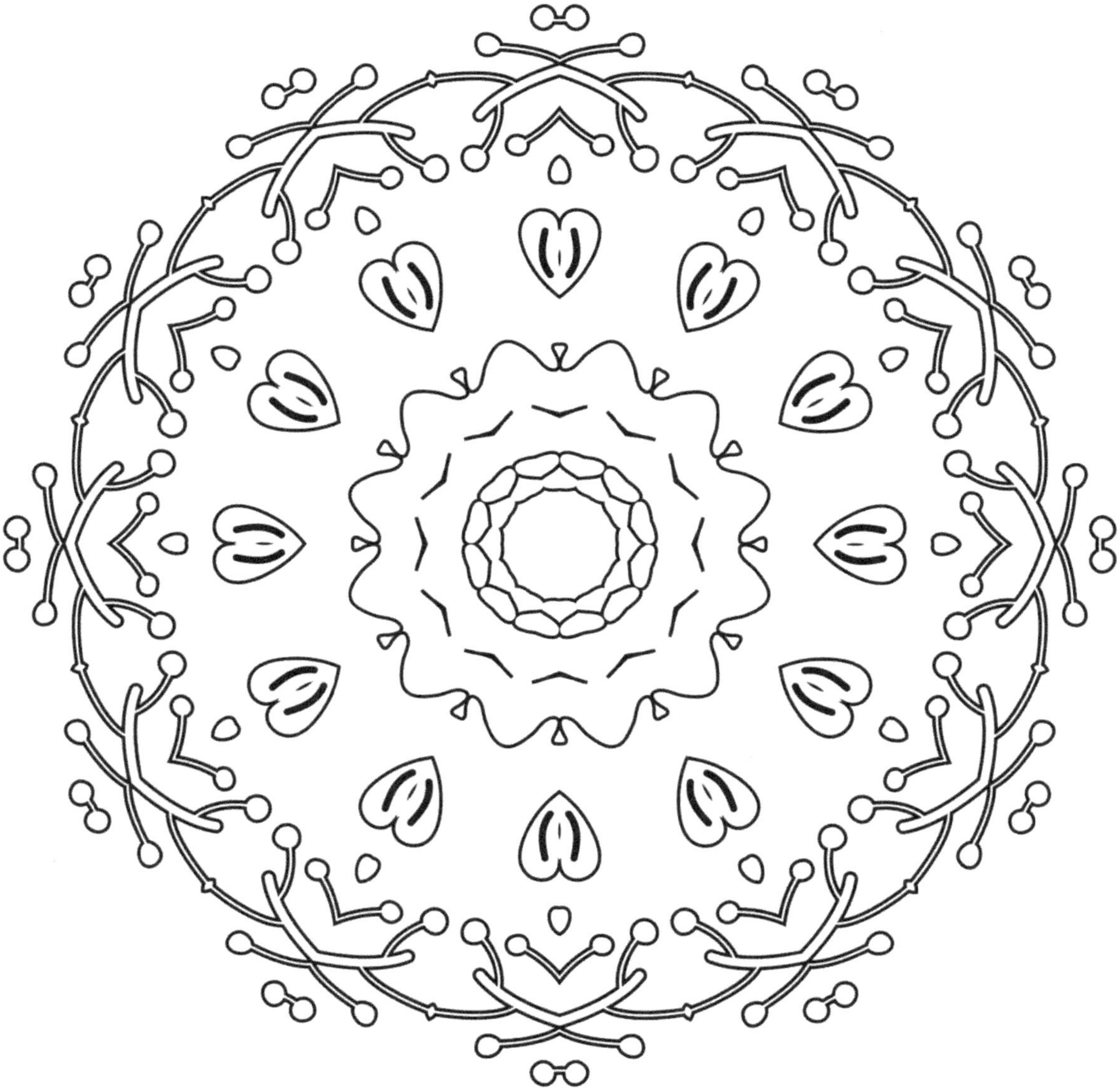

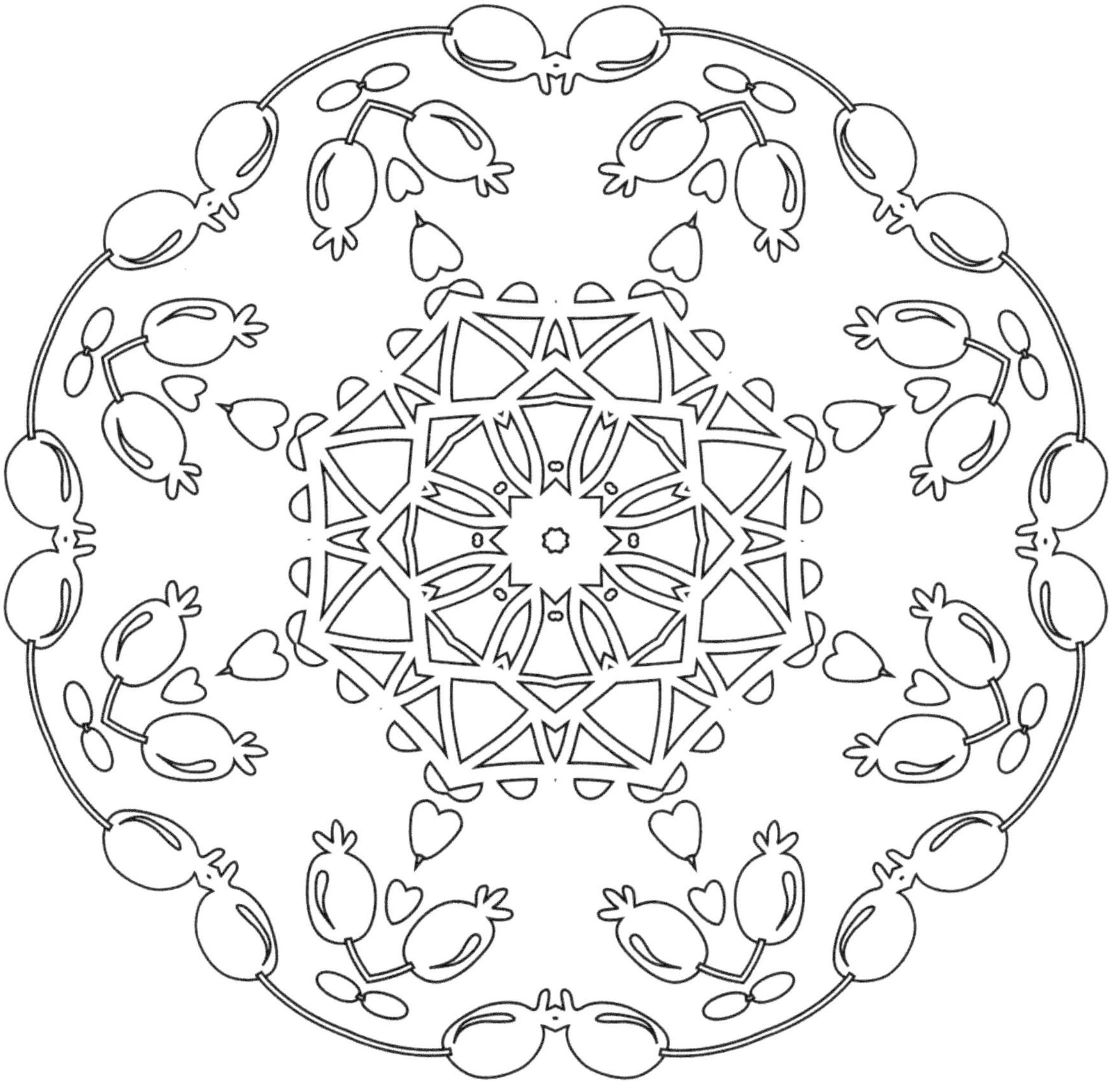

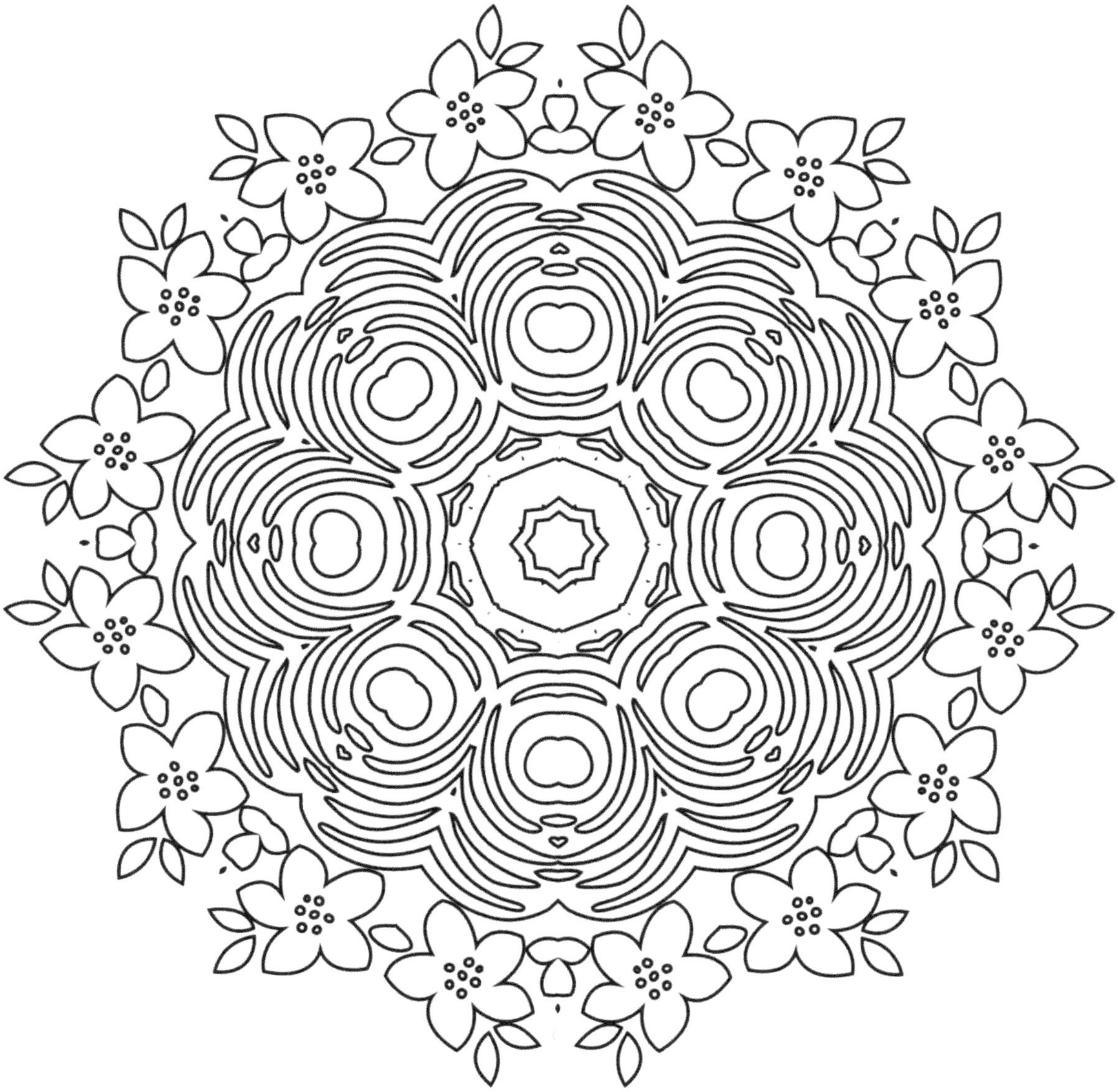

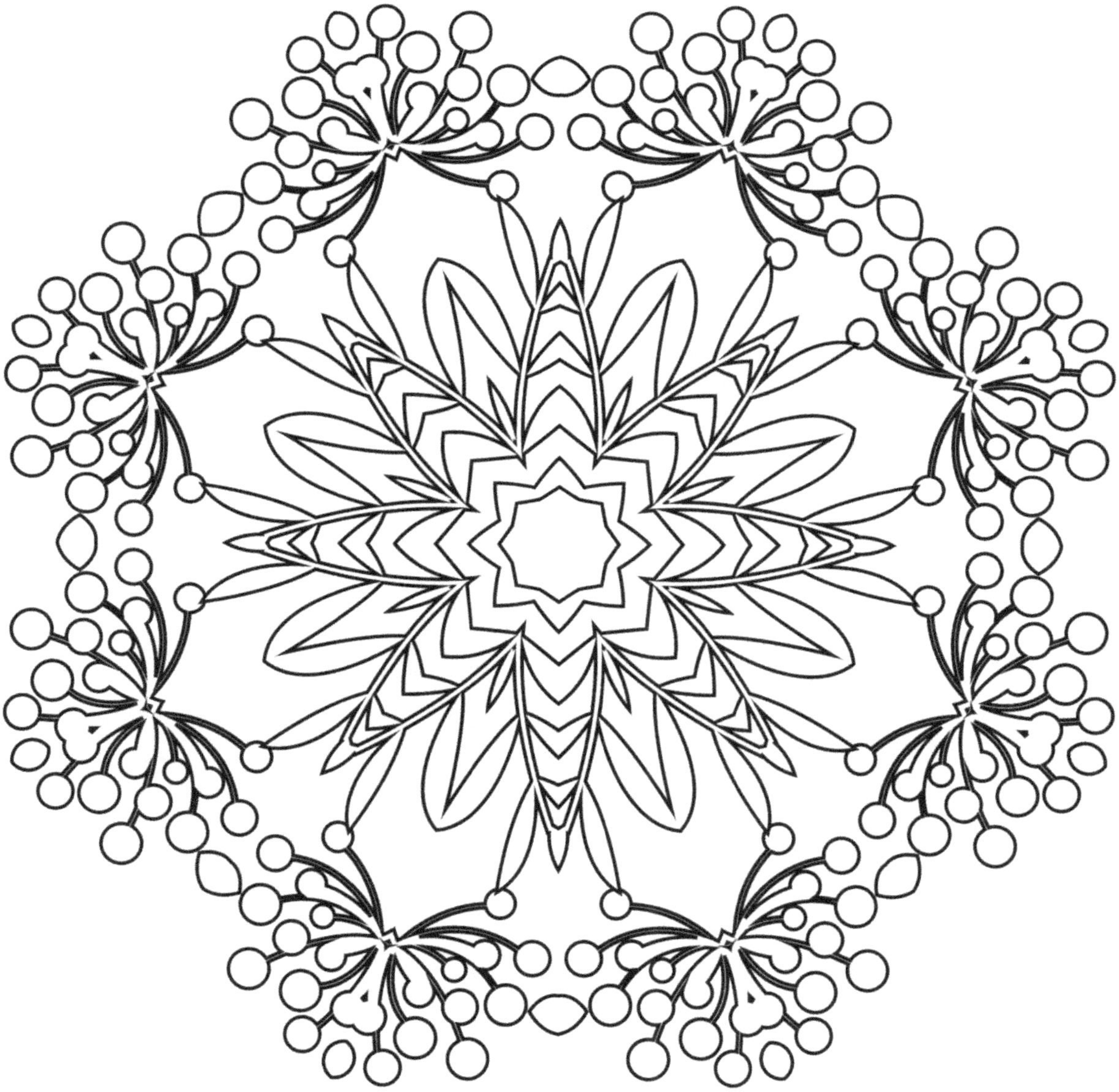

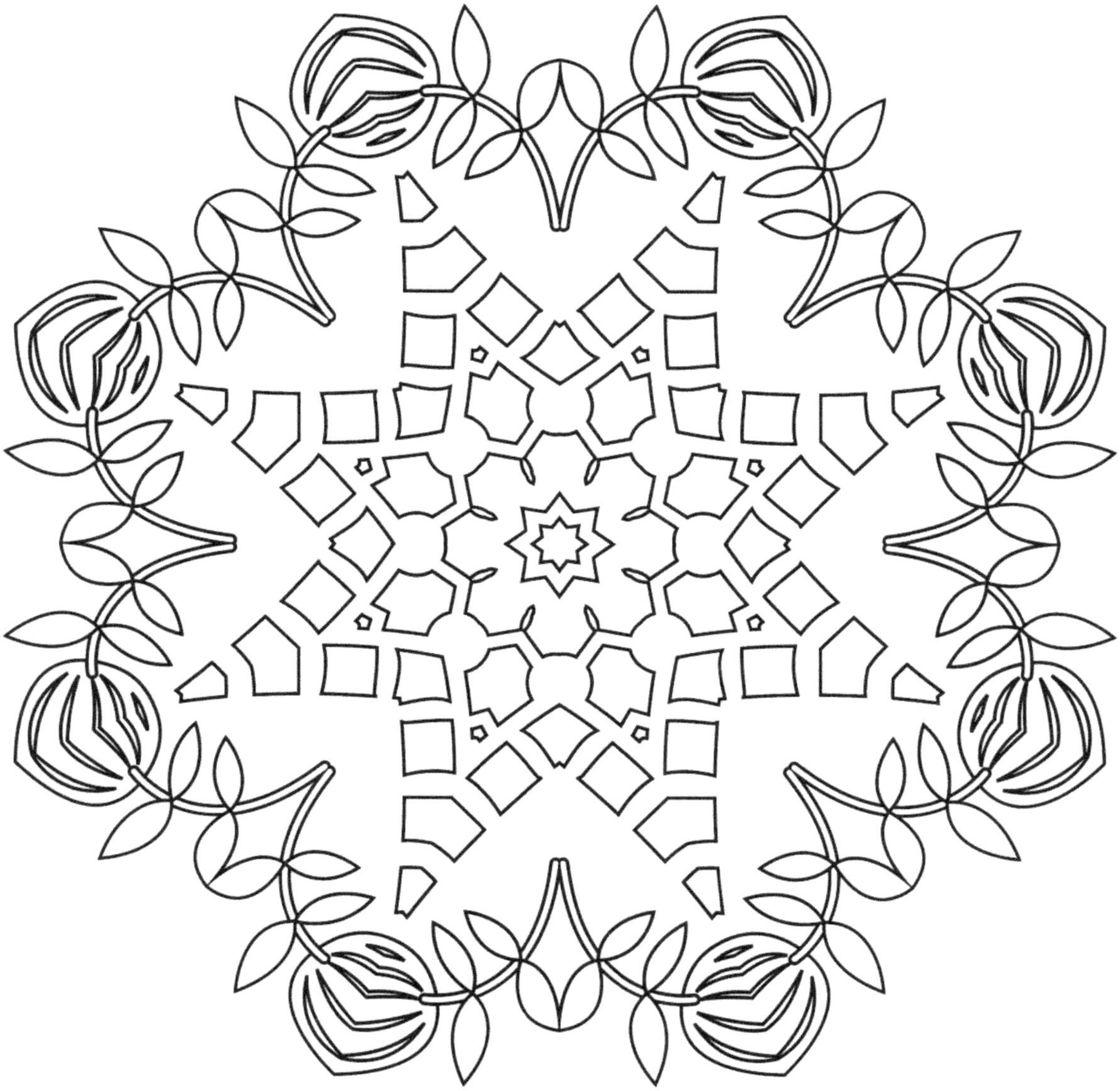

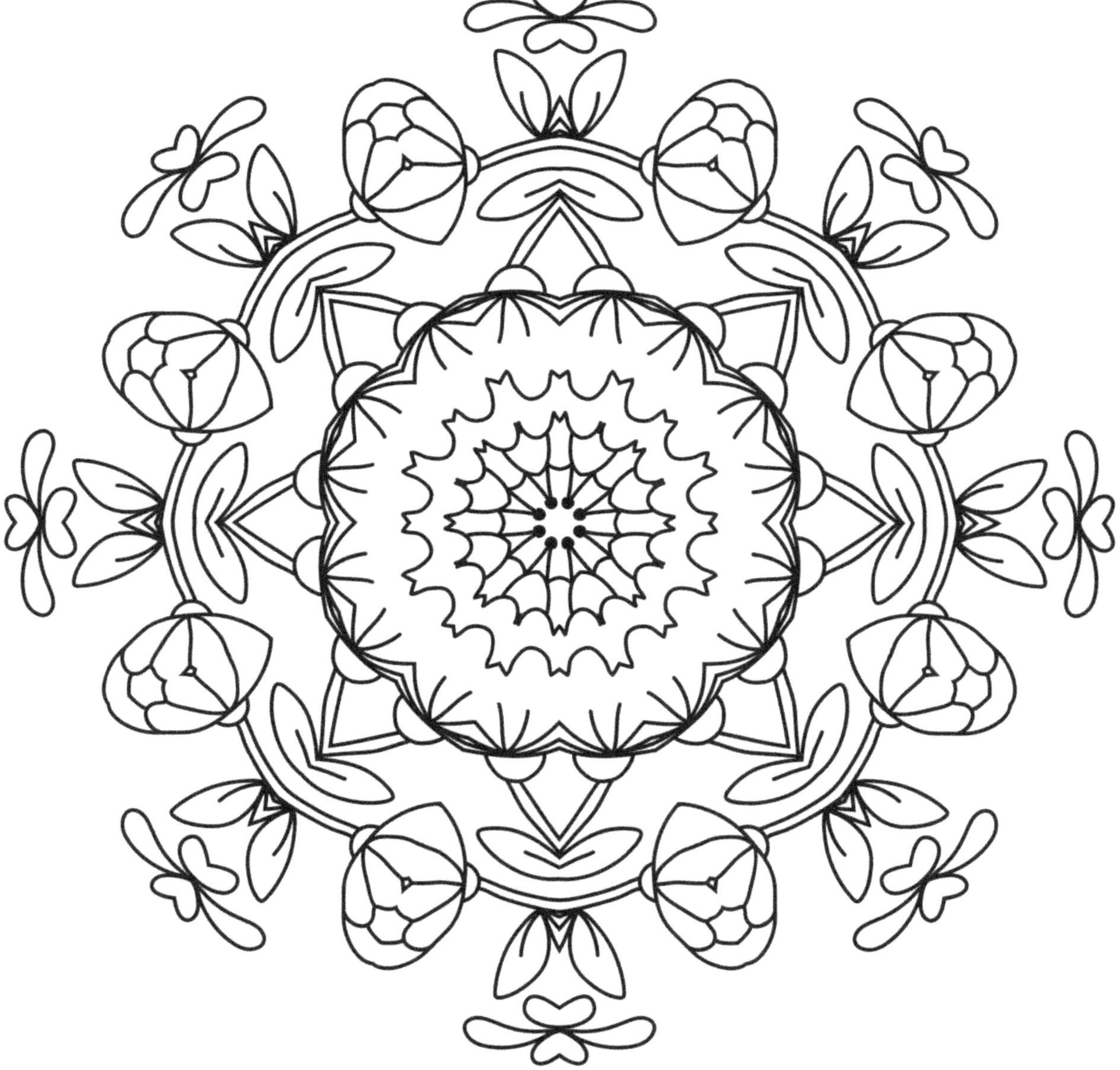

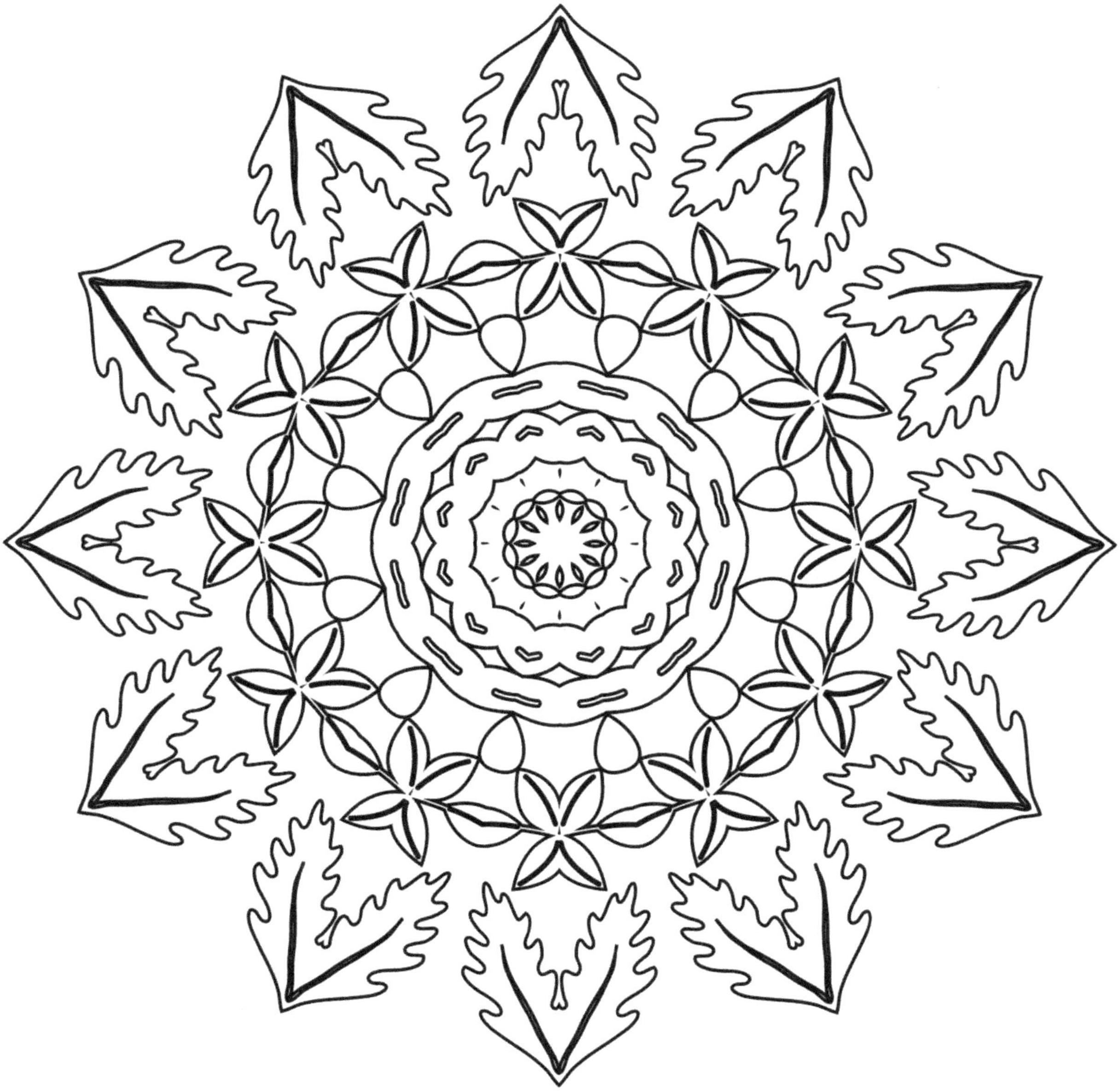

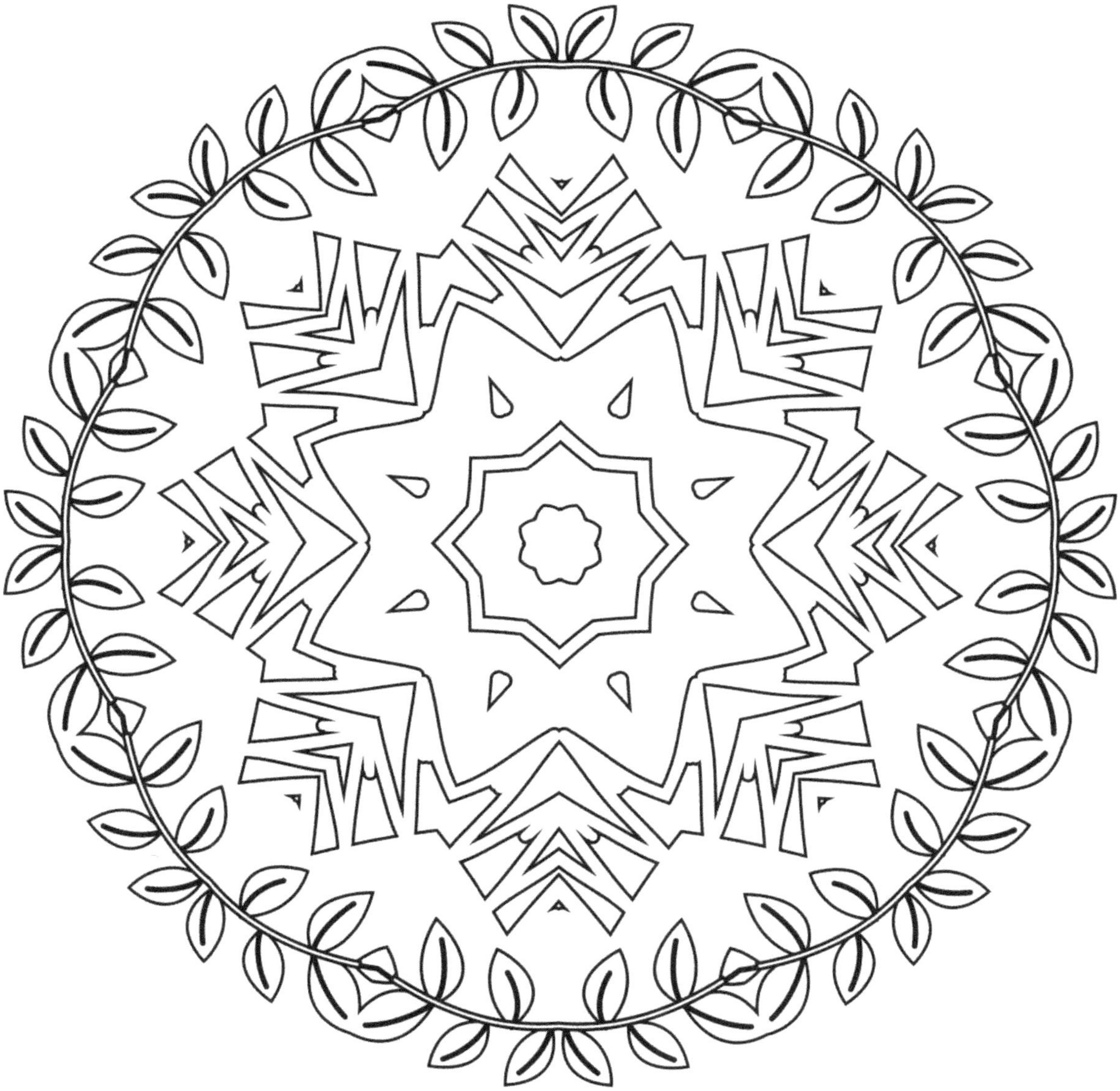

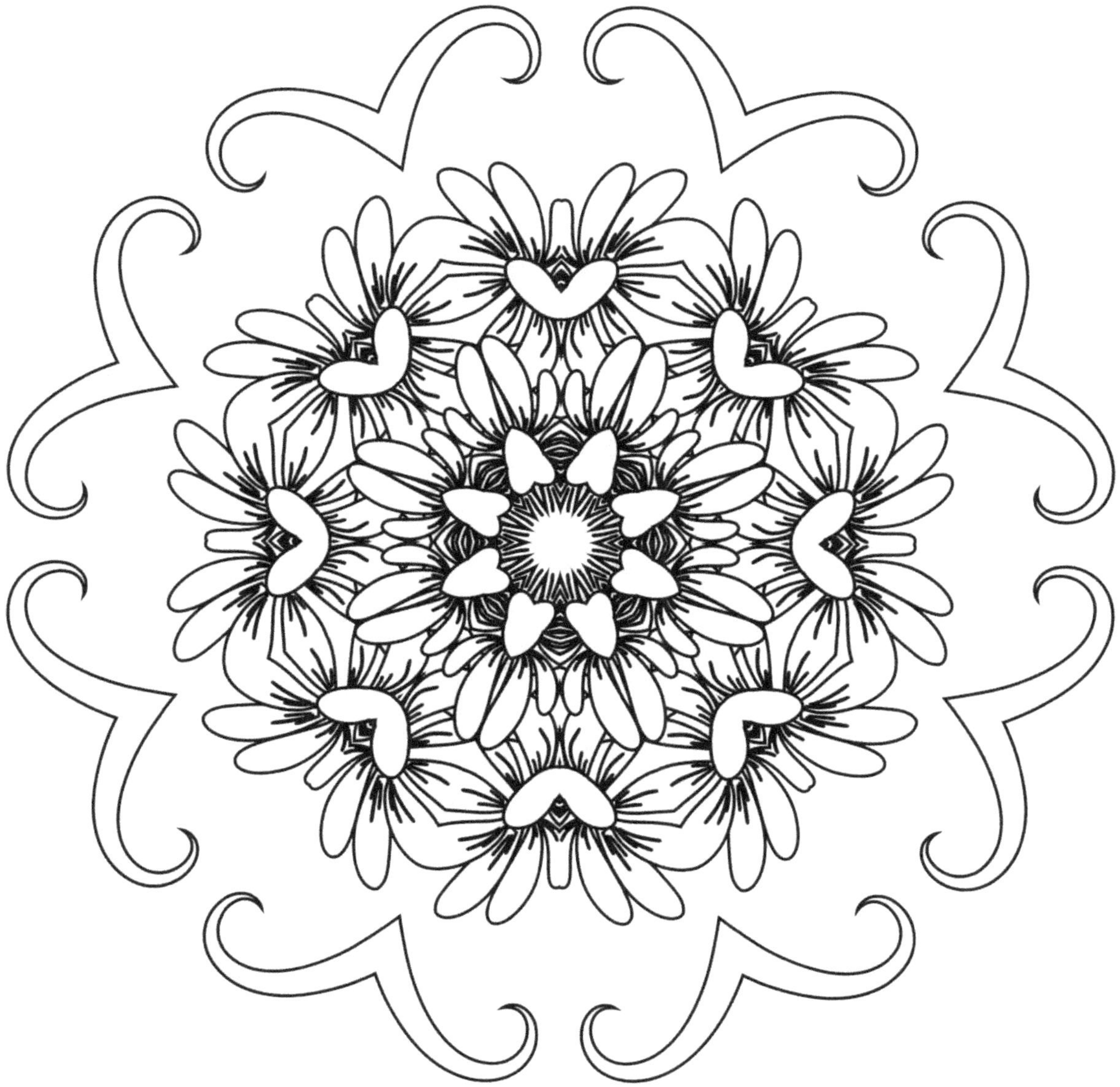

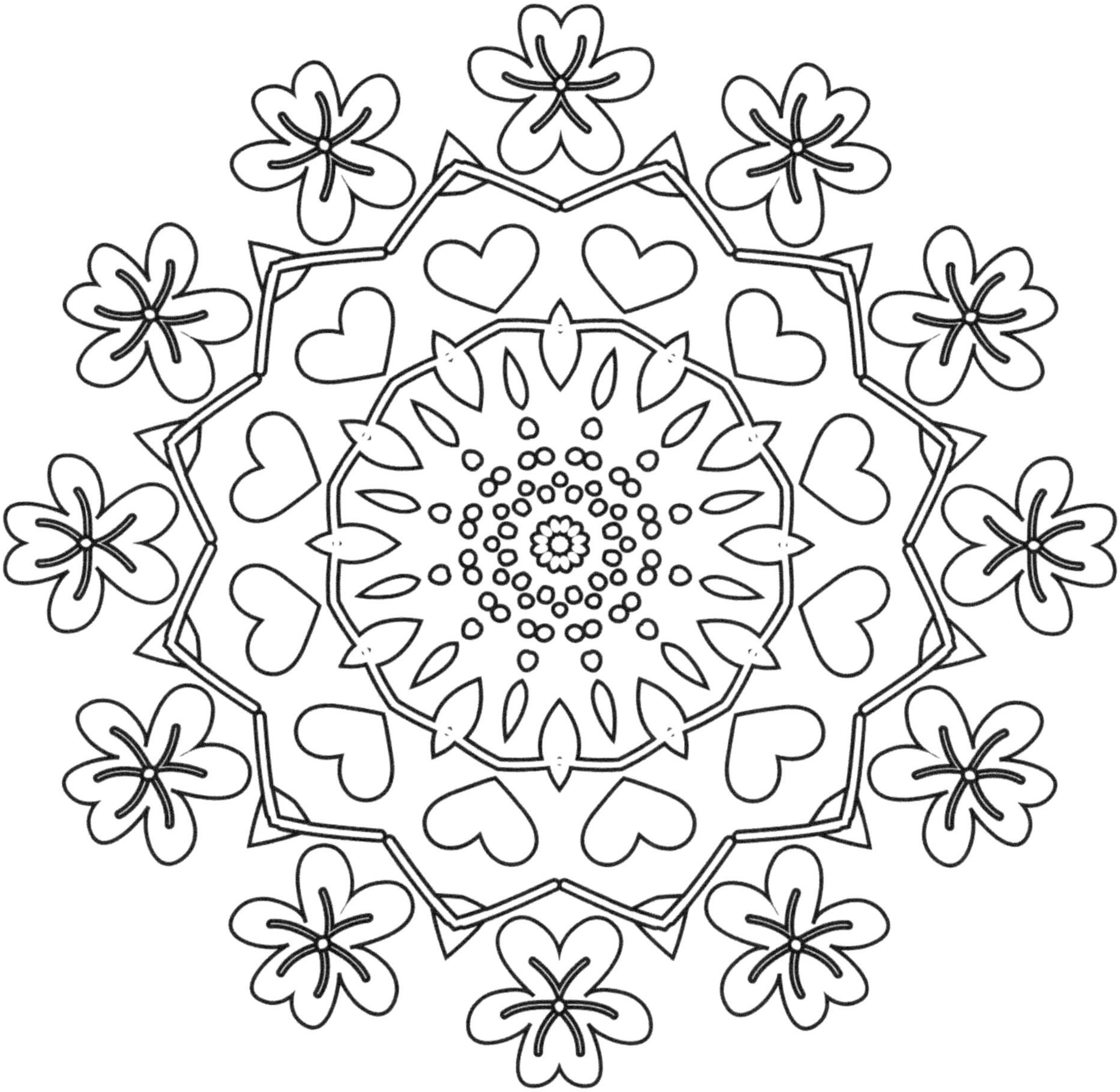

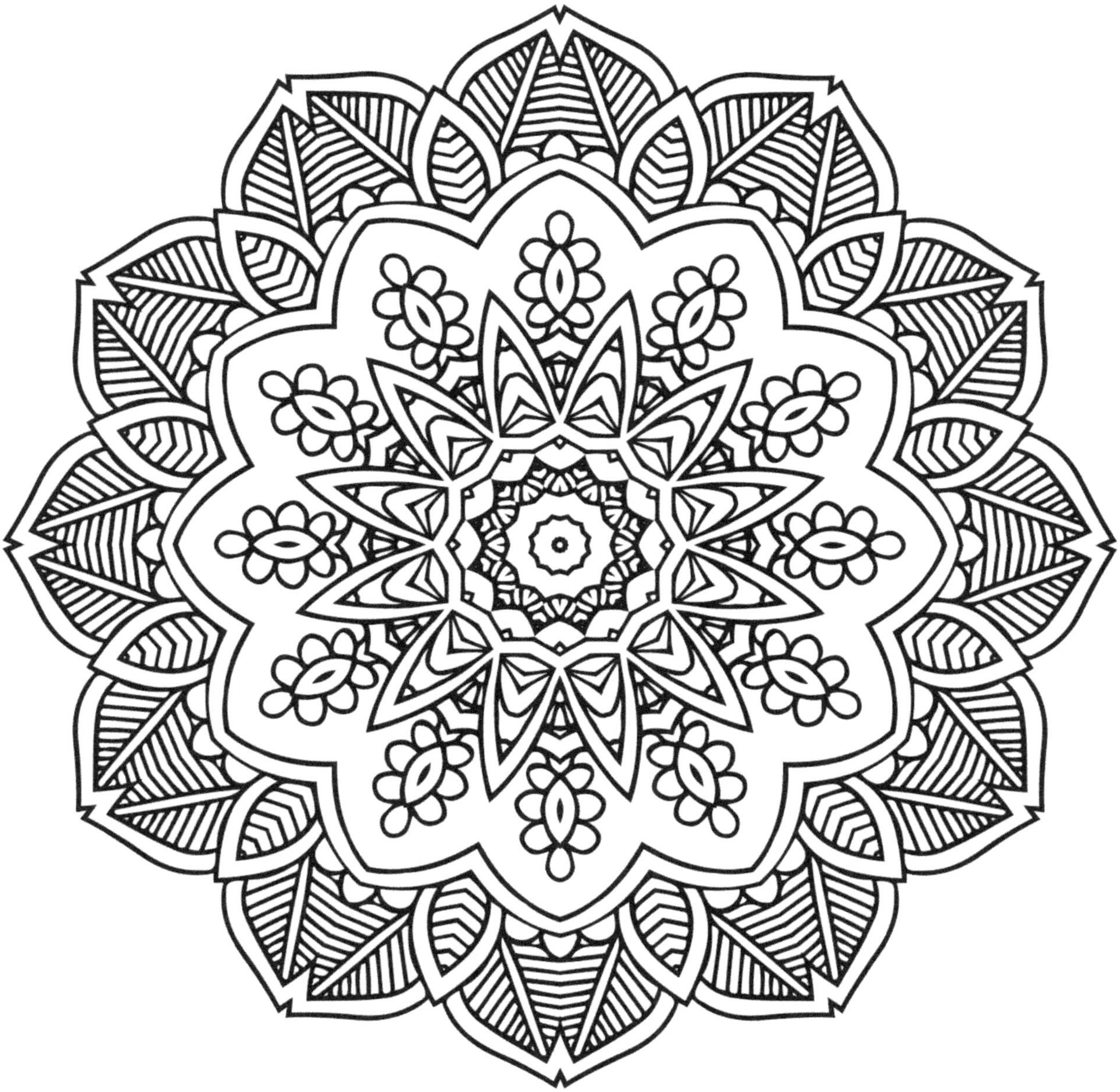

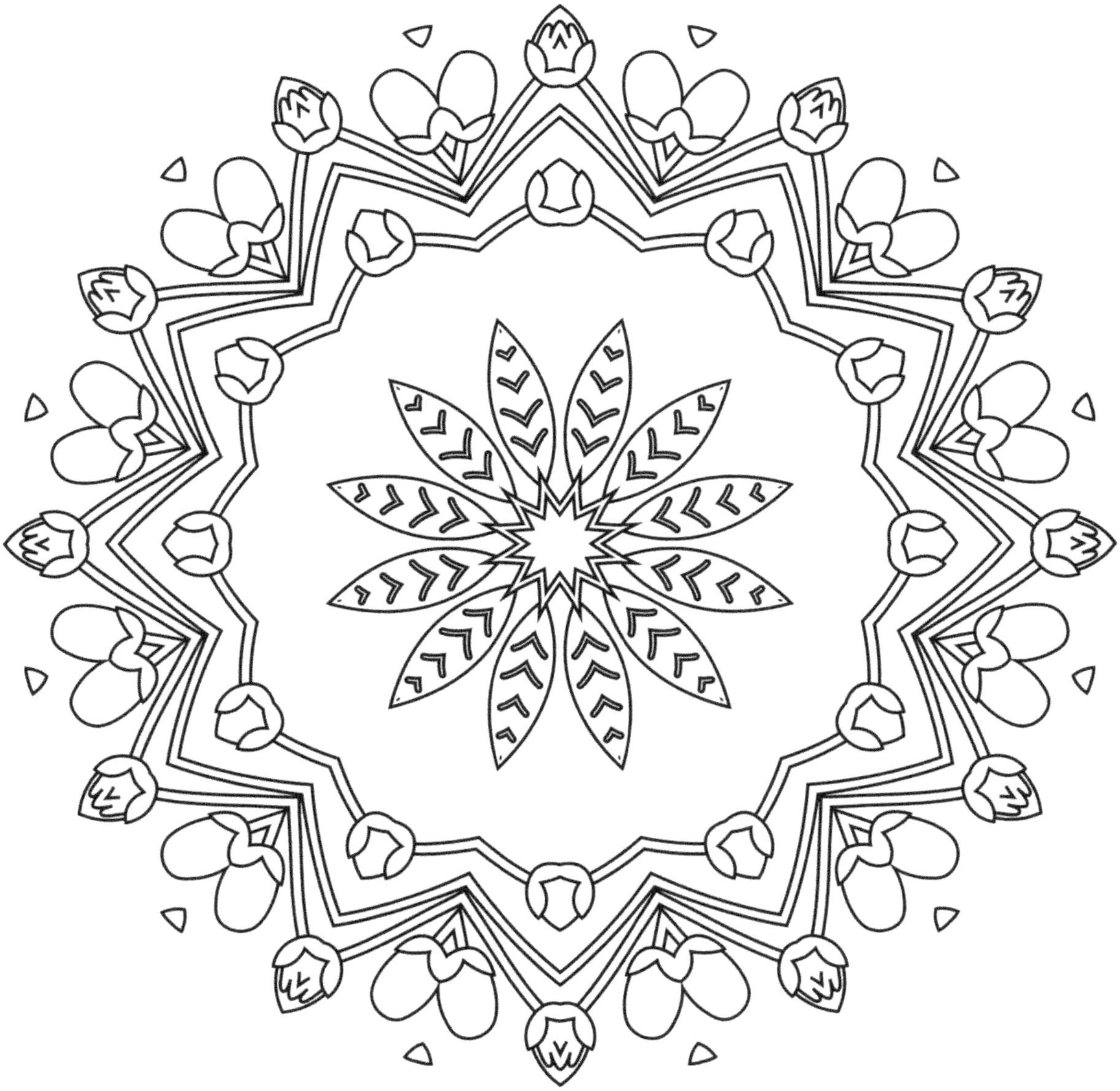

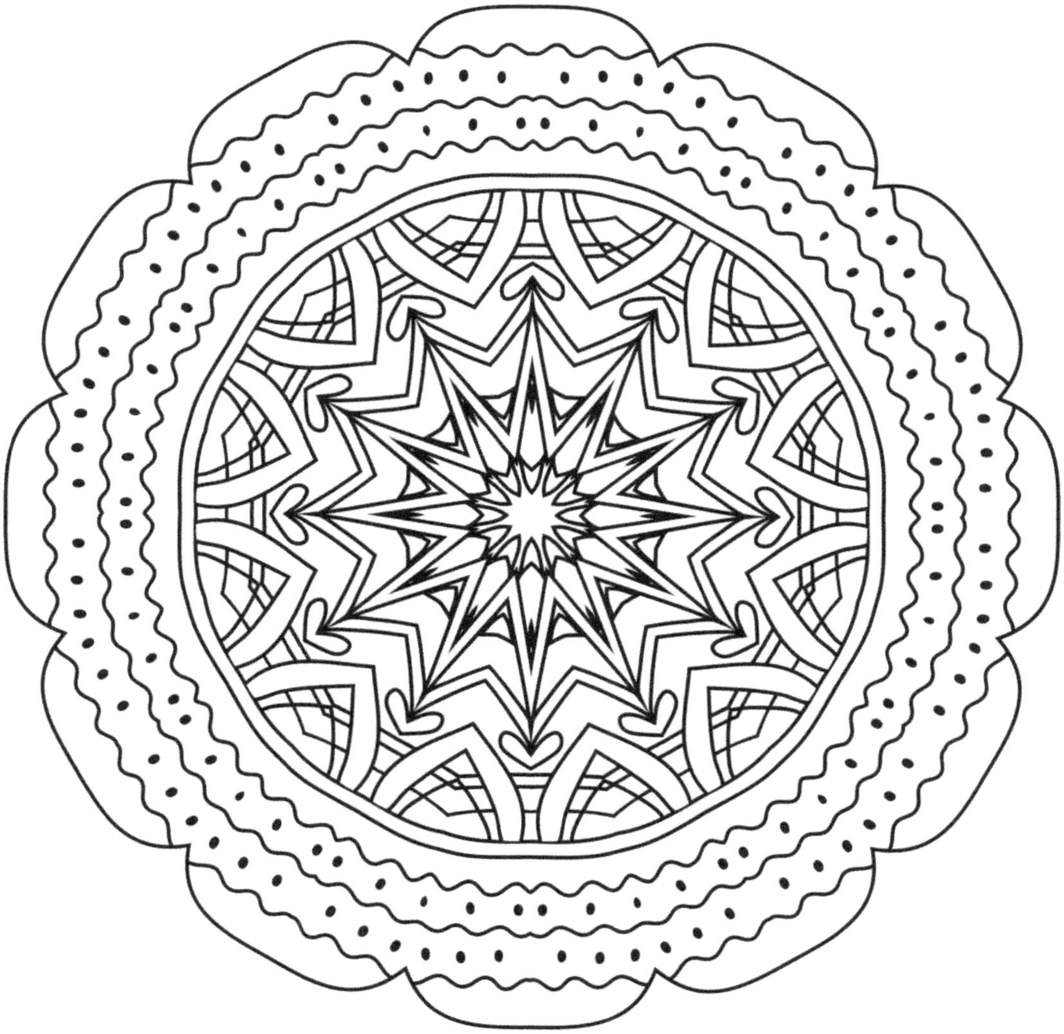

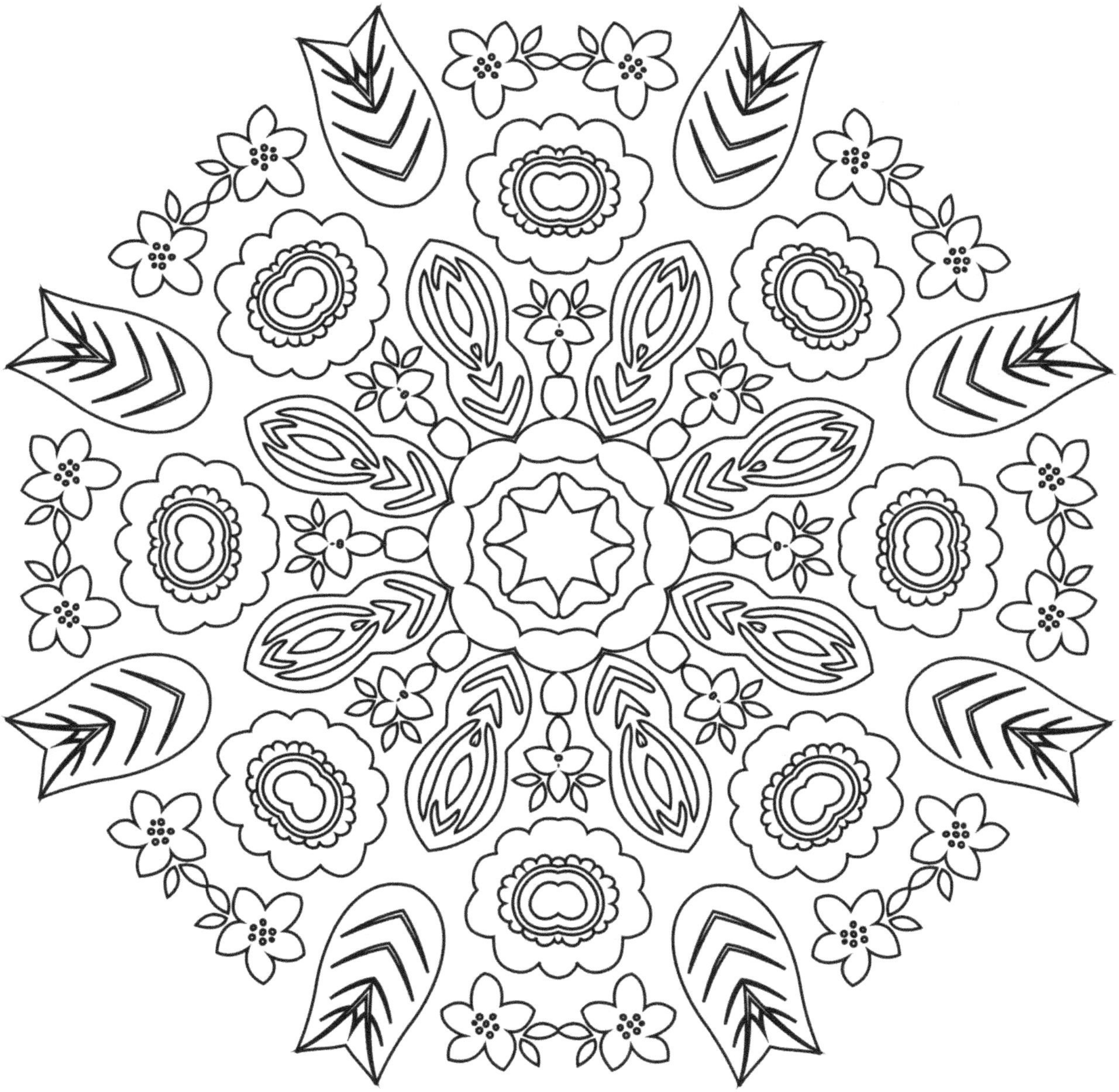

www.ingramcontent.com/pod-product-compliance
Lightning Source LLC
Chambersburg PA
CBHW080553190526
45169CB00007B/2764
9781539489054